KALAN

HOPE THESE WORDS
MAKE AN IMPACT IN
YOUR LIFE !

CREATING EFFICIENT FINANCIAL WEALTH

Gerardo Linarducci

Creating Efficient Financial Wealth

©2021 Gerardo Linarducci

print ISBN: 978-1-66780-787-4
ebook ISBN: 978-1-66780-788-1

CONTENTS

INTRODUCTION

Time to Make it Happen!

We are all on a financial journey. This journey began when our parents taught us the value of a dollar and the power that a dollar can have in society then, today, and years later.

By picking up this book, you have demonstrated that you have questions about the accumulation of money to have a better financial life when you decide to retire!

After all, isn't it the underlying premise that we are all saving money to have it and have the ability to enjoy our money, when we want to, how we want to, and with whom we want to?

As you read this book, I will be challenging your thought process about money, accumulating it, and the eroding factors that we have to deal with — such as taxes, inflation, and costs.

My parents and I immigrated to the United States in 1966. My parents Pasquale and Renee Linarducci, arrived in this country with very little money, no ability to communicate English, and not knowing how to read or write the language.

When writing this book, my father is 88, and my mother is 78 years old. Both are retired and living in Port St. Lucie, Florida.

I always say to myself, if these two individuals can make it in the USA, not having the ability of understanding, communicating in the early years of arrival, anyone can make it in life, if you want it bad enough. This is the example that my parents provided me, and I live that way every day, and I help my clients in the same manner as my parents.

To my devoted wife of thirty years, Jennifer, the gifts of support, unconditional love, and belief in me is something that I will always have and cherish today and every day.

To my two children, Sierra and Lorenzo. Without either of you in my life, I would have never had the opportunity to grow as much as I did, as a man, father, and supporter.

The two of you have and continue to make me a better person daily.

To my grandchildren Sage & Baby Lee that we welcome into this world in March, 2022. I hope that these words will have an impact on your life in the future.

I have the greatest job in the world. I honestly do not work and haven't worked in twenty-eight years. This industry is so gratifying and fulfilling to the human soul. Knowing that you are making a difference in someone's life is simply awesome. Many of my present clients have become friends; I want to spend time with them because they have the same family values as I do. Their wants, dreams, and desires are similar to mine.

CHAPTER 1

PHILOSOPHY

It was a beautiful sunny day during the fall of 1999 when a gentleman named Robert Castiglione said these words that impacted my thought process about money to this very day!

"Money is not Math, and Math is not Money." These words, twenty-three years later, speak the truth today as back then. I cannot stress this enough. This entire book is being written because of this philosophy.

Money is not a number. Money has value, and numbers represent that value. This is so important to understand. Adding dollars is very simple. $1+1 = 2$ / $3 \times 3 = 9$ / $10 \times 10 = 100$ These numbers represent the adding and multiplying of numbers. One dollar plus one dollar equals two dollars. That repents value. That has never changed and never will change. What will change is the purchasing power of those two dollars today, tomorrow, and twenty years from now. Not only will inflation play a factor, but how will taxes impact the final amount of what you keep?

Understanding how to ,*protect, save,* and *grow* your money from market fluctuation, taxes, inflation has been my mission since 1997.

As we begin to dive deeper into the philosophy of money, Newton's third law of physics states that an object at rest stays at rest, and an object in motion stays in motion. I want you to think about what you are doing with your money. Is it resting, or is it moving? The majority of us are keeping our money as a resting compounding account, regardless if it is a qualified or non-qualified account. It is simply growing because of the rate of return factor. It is at rest. Is this money gaining or losing value?

Having the right knowledge and skills, and focus. A majority of us have made financial decisions over our lifetime, at different times, during different economic times. Yet, we always fall back and think about money as a number and math, not as a value.

Building personal wealth is both an art and a science. To be successful, one must use various skills and tools to analyze potential outcomes, implement a strategy, and control the desired results.

Again money is not math, and math are not money. I hope by now you are beginning to understand this.

Coordinating these three steps is an ever-changing process due to variations in the economic circumstances surrounding one's personal life.

In my practice, I provide the client with the most efficient and cost-effective approach to building wealth and protecting their wealth as it grows.

We use an economic model that is called the "Protection, Savings, Growth Economic Model." This unique process focuses on the strategic positioning of your money over time. It helps us understand and determine all of your financial decisions and provides us a clearer and better understanding of correcting the issues that need to be addressed when it 5 Creating Efficient Financial Wealth comes to protecting, saving, growing their wealth, along with cash flow, and personal debt.

The goal is to create new opportunities for you that we could not identify because our money decisions were not coordinated or integrated. Add additional benefits of wealth building, improved management of your money, and potential tax savings. So, I want you to think about what tool you are using in your financial life that will assist you in organizing all of your money decisions on one page?

Many people today have used financial apps that are available to coordinate their accounts, but very few APPS help you integrate the asset you own to make a more efficient money decision.

I want you to think of an x-ray. Your x-ray is just one slide. That is it. An x-ray can be taken in different angles, but the main one focuses on the physical issue you are having. This is how I work with my clients. I use a tool that will develop your own financial x-ray reading your personal financial issues.

Without an Economic based Model, certain inefficient occurrences may happen to your assets. These assets can become uncoordinated, non-intergraded, based on opinion, limited to wants and needs, limited to certain financial goals, purchased because of convenience, and many times these assets are not accessible.

By having a very well-structured Economic Model , you can coordinate, integrate your assets, based on facts, designed well beyond needs and goals, Strategies that are very simple to integrate, and a majority of the time, assets are accessible.

The Protection, Savings and Growth model is not used to accumulate wealth, rather the Model is used to identify areas of non-efficient money use, and we can work together as a team to adjust and get better results for you! Below you will find a version of a blank PS&G Model. The model is also used to organize your personal financial life.

PRESENT POSITION

Date

Name   Age

Occupation   Income

Total Income

% of Income Saved

Total Assets

Debt

Debt Type	Rate	Months Left	Monthly Payment	Unpaid Balance

TOTAL

Additional Information

Vehicle Insurance	Property Insurance	Liability Insurance	PROTECTION
Disability Insurance	Medical Insurance	Government Plans	
Wills & Documents	Trusts & Ownership	Life Insurance	
WCA/Checking	Savings	Credit Union	
Savings Bonds	Certificates	Money Market	
Tax Deferred	Tax Free	Tax Deductible	
Government Bonds	Corporate Bonds	Municipal Bonds	GROWTH
Preferred Stocks	Blue Chip Stocks	Growth Securities	
Collectibles	Real Estate	Business/Shelters	

CHAPTER 2

BALANCE OF ECONOMIC POWERS

We all generally have one thirty-to-forty-year cycle to save for retirement income. Please pay close attention. I said retirement income. Most of us have a retirement savings plan, not a retirement income plan. There is a major difference between the two.

The major questions that your financial professional should ask are: #1 How much do you need to save? #2 Where do we deposit those savings dollars? The first question pertains to the volume of annual savings you would do, and the second pertains to allocating those savings for efficiency to create your retirement income in the future. The second question needs to be addressed before the first.... Until you know the efficiency of your retirement income planning strategies, it is futile to try and determine how much to save. For example, the less efficient your strategy, the more you have to save to reach your retirement income goal.

There are two economic strategies to consider for the efficiency of your retirement income planning. This first is the Accumulation of your money. This is driven by the short-term fluctuating interest rates and is generally provided by the investment-based vehicles. The second is the distribution strategy which is driven by the power of actuarial science and is generally provided by the insurance-based vehicles.

Prior to the 1980s these strategies were balanced automatically to create people's retirement income through the defined benefit pension plans for most people.

Today, most people are only getting the accumulation power by default. They need to know how to incorporate the distribution strategy back into their financial lives for the efficiency of retirement income planning.

Where to put it?

Efficiency is lost if either power is weighed down too much or in either direction. We must create a two economic strategy balanced for maximum efficiency.

Once efficiency for savings allocations has been understood, the next questions is, "How much to save?" This is generally a matter of trying to match your income during your working years, and lifestyle with the retirement lifestyle you desire in the future.

During your accumulation period, your working years, the annual savings someone is doing generally comes out of their annual income and then the remainder is what creates their current lifestyle. If you save too little during your accumulation period or allocate it inefficiently, you could have a lifestyle shortage in retirement.

If you save more than needed out of your income, these could have reduced your lifestyle in your accumulation's years to the point where you would have a lifestyle jump or surplus at retirement age.

Normally, people are looking to set an annual savings amount that matches their early working year's lifestyle to be close to their future retirement income lifestyle.

Retirement income planning centers around solving these two questions for everyone.

The last thing that we must discuss is the type of legacy that you want to leave behind. So many people leave whatever is left. Our goal is to provide you the opportunity to enjoy every dollar that you have saved during your working years and spend every one prior to your passing. At your passing have all these dollars replaced, and redeposited into your beneficiary's account. Tax free.

I would like for you to take a moment, pause the reading, and think about this...

How many years did you work? How many events did you miss? How much overtime did you put in? Now you have retired, and the main question on your mind is, I hope I saved enough for my money to last. Your accumulation number needs to do several things at this point. Here they are:

1. These dollars need to provide you an income.

2. Provide an income for my spouse or partner when I am gone.

3. I have limited availability to use these dollars because it could potentially reduce the following years income if I do.

4. What's left behind on the second passing is the legacy that I leave behind.

The question that I raise most of the time is, why did you work and suffer all those years, missing those events and functions, and not enjoying your money?

Why not have the ability to spend every dime you saved, and let an insurance company replace all the money that you enjoyed, and create an ever-lasting legacy, and leave the world a better place than when you entered it decades ago!

CHAPTER 3

ACCUMULATE RATE AND THE DISTRIBUTION RATE

Newton's First Law of Motion states that a body at rest will remain at rest unless an outside force acts on it, and a body in motion at a constant velocity will remain in motion in a straight line unless acted upon by an outside force.

Compounding and accumulating your money. This is the analogy I want you to think about as you read this chapter.

I want you to visualize in your mind two things. #1 A pond. This pond is at rest. It can be anywhere. You must understand that a pond has no running water, and it fills with natural water and run-off water. Because there is no running water, life grows in this pond. Bacteria, weeds, grass, and so forth. The pond is going to represent your money. And the bacteria, weeds, etc., are going to be what erodes your money over time; they are taxes and inflation.

Now I want you to think about a running stream. The stream is fresh, the stream has life, but good life, fish, all different kinds of fish, depending on its location. The river stream is your money. Now that your money is moving, it can grow, grow at an efficient pace.

Now I want you to think about your accumulation rate of money. What does this mean? Accumulation of money? Is it the savings of your dollars into a certain account? Is it the rate of return that you are earning? Could it be both? The answer is *yes* to all of the above.

We must explore much deeper when it comes to the accumulation of money. We must think about what can erode our money while it accumulates as well. Things like taxes today, taxes in the future, price of goods today, and the inflation of goods. How is technology going to play out with new consumer goods, like the electric car? 2035 is just fourteen years away, and this could happen during your accumulation years? How much is this going to cost?

How about the replacement of consumer goods? As these items begin to break down, do they need to be replaced for us to survive in the world? What number iPhones will be available by 2035, and most importantly at what cost? I want you to challenge yourself and think back just a short few years ago. Most of us had the big bag phone, then it went to the car phone, with the antenna. Then it was the Motorola Flip handheld phone, then the Blackberry, then came Apple, the original iPhone, and all the iPhones that followed. How many of these phones did you purchase? To keep up with technology, we must update our products, so that we can function daily.

Where will technology be by the year 2035, and at what cost will it be? Every dollar that you put into this technology is a dollar that will not be a factor in your accumulation rate.

We must understand the ins and outs of how the money will accumulate in the most effective and efficient way possible for us to have any chance of living the retirement lifestyle that we desire.

By accumulating money for retirement, you will have a chance! But now, we need to explore what the future holds when outcomes to taxes. How do we teach ourselves about this? One way, not the only way, of course, is by just looking back at what tax rates have been over the past twenty, twenty-five, thirty years, and see where taxes are today, what are the expenses of this country, how much money is the government taking in, and then, try to figure out how much of the bill we as Americans are going to be responsible for in paying with our tax dollars.

As I write this book, we are in the second phase of the Covid-19 Delta variant. How is this going to play out in the long term regarding the financial impact of our government spending?

So, we must think about more than the rate of return of the earning of our money. I hope by this point you are beginning to understand that there is so much more than a "+" sign or a "×" by the dollar to give us a balance in a column of a spreadsheet. The number! Not a value!

Everything about accumulating money for retirement, but the question that I rarely hear is, what type of income would you like to have when you retire? How important should inflation be in our planning? Income plays a very important role during retirement. Another question that I love to ask the people that I meet with? Regarding your retirement assets, what type of income would you like to have in retirement?

If you cannot reach the same income level at retirement, how much of your lifestyle are you willing to give up and change. I thought you were supposed to enjoy your golden years, not give things up, and not enjoy yourself. Please help me understand this traditional thinking? I hope this makes sense.

Many of us have searched online for a compound interest calculator and have entered the following economic formula to create and generate wealth. This is the formula.

M × R × T = W (Money multiplied by time multiplied by the rate of return = wealth.) Now we understand the formula. Let us take a much closer look and see what the **numbers** look like.

For this example, I will use a single lump sum deposit of $10,000, With an interest-earning rate of six percent on average, over thirty years period.

The following calculator proves, in theory, to be correct. $57,435. Please validate these numbers yourself.

Years	Opening Balance	Interest Earned	Ending Balance
1	$10,000	6%	$10,600
2	$10,600	6%	$11,236
3	$11,236	6%	$11,910
4	$11,910	6%	$12,625
5	$12,625	6%	$13,382
6	$13,382	6%	$14,185
7	$14,185	6%	$15,036
8	$15,036	6%	$15,938
9	$15,938	6%	$16,895
10	$16,895	6%	$17,908
11	$17,908	6%	$18,983
12	$18,983	6%	$20,122
13	$20,122	6%	$21,329
14	$21,329	6%	$22,609
15	$22,609	6%	$23,966
16	$23,966	6%	$25,404

17	$25,404	6%	$26,928
18	$26,928	6%	$28,543
19	$28,543	6%	$30,256
20	$30,256	6%	$32,071
21	$32,071	6%	$33,996
22	$33,996	6%	$36,065
23	$36,065	6%	$38,197
24	$38,197	6%	$40,489
25	$40,489	6%	$42,919
26	$42,919	6%	$45,494
27	$45,494	6%	$48,223
28	$48,223	6%	$51,117
29	$51,117	6%	$54,184
30	$54,184	6%	$57,435

Now the fun begins! What are the costs that you incurred because you have been compounding in a non-qualified account?

1. Is there a tax cost that needs to be considered? YEP. Remember the erosion of wealth discussion earlier?

2. Because you are paying a tax that you really did not have to, you now have incurred a "Lost Opportunity Cost" Another wealth eroding factor.

The definition of "Lost Opportunity Cost" is not only giving up that dollar but also giving up the ability to earn interest with that dollar.

So, let's have some more fun with the calculator. Now we see some of the costs that are involved with compounding. Taxes and Lost Opportunity Costs (L.O.C).

Let's add the tax cost into the equation. Marginal twenty percent. If you look at the annual tax column, you will now see the compounding of the tax year after year after year.

Now let's add the lost opportunity cost into the equation. Four percent. The numbers are far worse.

Remember, it's not about where to put your money, but more about how I should put my money.

In total, you have a gross worth of $57,435 with expenses totaling in Taxes and L.O.C of $15,601.

Years	Opening Balance	Interest Earned	Taxes	Cumulative Balance	End Balance
1	$10,000	6%	$-120.00	$-125.00	$10,600
2	$10,600	6%	$-127.00	$-262.00	$11,236
3	$11,236	6%	$-135.00	$-413.00	$11,910
4	$11,910	6%	$-143.00	$-578.00	$12,625
5	$12,625	6%	$-151.00	$-759.00	$13,382
6	$13,382	6%	$-161.00	$-956.00	$14,185
7	$14,185	6%	$-170.00	$-1171.00	$15,036
8	$15,036	6%	$-180.00	$-1406.00	$15,938
9	$15,938	6%	$-191.00	$-1661.00	$16,895
10	$16,895	6%	$-203.00	$-1938.00	$17,908
11	$17,908	6%	$-215.00	$-2239.00	$18,983
12	$18,983	6%	$-228.00	$-2566.00	$20,122
13	$20,122	6%	$-241.00	$-2919.00	$21,329
14	$21,329	6%	$-256.00	$-3302.00	$22,609
15	$22,609	6%	$-271.00	$-3717.00	$23,966
16	$23,966	6%	$-288.00	$-4164.00	$25,404
17	$25,404	6%	$-305.00	$-4648.00	$26,928
18	$26,928	6%	$-323.00	$-5170.00	$28,543
19	$28,543	6%	$-343.00	$-5733.00	$30,256
20	$30,256	6%	$-363.00	$-6340.00	$32,071
21	$32,071	6%	$-385.00	$-6994.00	$33,996
22	$33,996	6%	$-408.00	$-7698.00	$36,065
23	$36,065	6%	$-432.00	$-8455.00	$38,197
24	$38,197	6%	$-458.00	$-9270.00	$40,489
25	$40,489	6%	$-486.00	$-10,146.00	$42,919
26	$42,919	6%	$-515.00	$-11,088.00	$45,494

27	$45,494	6%	$-546.00	$-12,099.00	$48,223
28	$48,223	6%	$-579.00	$-13,185.00	$51,117
29	$51,117	6%	$-613.00	$-14,350.00	$54,184
30	$54,184	6%	$-650.00	$-15,601.00	$57,435

The million-dollar question, now if there were specific money strategies to help you reduce the amount of tax that is owed and then recapture some of the L.O.C would you not want to know about it?

There are proven money tax reduction strategies out there. These strategies have worked for hundreds of my clients and can work for you as well.

The success of these tax-saving strategies, depends on you having an open mind to these outside the box thought processes.

To obtain better and more efficient results, you cannot use the same thought process, that you have used in the past. You will never be able to get a different result. You must have a different thought process when using these proven strategies.

CHAPTER 4

AVERAGE RATES OF RETURNS VS. ACTUAL RATES OF RETURNS

This chapter is where the fun begins! I MEAN REALLY BEGINS! Let me begin by explaining, and I am not here saying I can actually generate these types of returns for you. These are for educational purposes only, and no return or interest guarantee is made nor suggested.

Example 1. $10,000 Balance, four-year period, with a twenty-five percent return? What is your answer?

A = $24,414

B = $10,000

What would you say if I proved to you both answers are correct? Review the calculator below, or better yet, go and create your own spreadsheet, or find a calculator online, and go for it! Look at your results. VERY INTERESTING!

Year

1	$10,000	25%	=	$12,500	YES
2	$12,500	25%	=	$15,625	NICE
3	$15,625	25%	=	$19,531	KEEP IT GOING
4	$19,531	25%	=	**$24,414**	CAN'T BELIEVE IT

25% Average rate of return

Or

Year

1	$10,000	100%	=	$20,000	Awesome Gain
2	$20,000	-50%	=	$10,000	Ouch that hurt
3	$10,000	100%	=	$20,000	I'm back in the game
4	$20,000	-50%	=	**$10,000**	**What?**

25% Average rate of return

Both answers are correct! You must understand that the number you see is only the average rate of return. Not the actual rate of return.

In another example. This time we are going to use a zero percent rate of return. Can you lose any of your money if your statement shadows an average of zero percent? Is it remotely possible to lose money with a zero percent average rate of return?

Year

1	$10,000	0%	=	$10,000	
2	$10,000	0%	=	**$10,000**	ZERO PERCENT AVERAGE R.O.R

Actual Loss of 0%

Year

1	$10,000	7%	=	$10,700	
2	$10,700	-7%	=	**$9,951**	ZERO PERCENT AVERAGE R.O.R

Actual loss of (-.25%)

Have I gotten your mind thinking yet? Do you think with a better understanding between the difference of average vs. actual rates of return? Would it make a difference in your financial life economically today and in the future?

How can we get the right solutions when you start with the wrong premise? Our financial and retirement lifestyles depend on this, yet most of us have no clue what is being done to us.

Please, please. Use the average rate of return only as a tool to measure the results. The average will get you close to your goal.

Imagine all the decisions you have made in the past because you were always thinking about the average rate of return.

What could you have done differently now that you have this valuable information? How much better could you presently be financial if you were not caught in this trap?

One final Example for you. I want you to understand that the average rate of return could be your worst nightmare.

Ten-thousand-dollar deposit for two years with a twenty percent R.O.R. what is your answer? Don't spoil it. Do the math, then check your answers.

A = $1,440

B = $1,280

C = $800

Example

Year 1	Year 2	Average ROR	Ending Balance
20%	20%	20%	$1,440
60%	-20%	20%	$1,280
100%	-60%	20%	$800

What did you come up with? These are all correct answers. So, I challenge you to start and begin thinking outside the box. This information must be told, and explained, and educated to our youth.

How do you feel at this very moment, now that you have just learned something new when it comes to money and math?

When This was demonstrated to me, it hit me smack in the face, and it hurt, it hurt bad.

I feel sorry for the individuals that do not know what they do not know. I hope now you know something you didn't know just fifteen minutes prior!

The internet is a very powerful tool to use to help you find information. But the question is, how can you find the information you need if you don't know what you are looking for?

CHAPTER 5

WEALTH TRANSFERS

On a beautiful warm winter day, in the middle of January 2002, I attended a financial symposium in Las Vegas. Yes, I went to the symposium and paid attention! I heard these words. These words have forever changed how I think about finances and the legacy I want to leave behind.

These words are so important that they can and will change the course of your life and legacy.

Read them over twice or three times to let them sink in.

These are the notes that I took, and I want to share them with you.

If I could tell you the exact day that your retirement account would suffer its greatest losses, would you want to know that day?

Then knowing that day, if you could do something about it now to prevent those losses, would you do it?

I will be going over the following potential wealth transfers that each one of us could have.

- Taxes
- Tax refunds

These transfers can create financial losses for you. I cannot express the importance of working with a professional who understands these transfers, and determine how they could or will affect you. There is so much more to transfer than what we see on the surface.

Let's explore these four transfers. By the way, these are my favorites, and I share these wealth transfers in my practice daily with present and future clients, that want to make a change and make a difference in their lives, and the lives of the people that they care about the most.

Taxes:

If you knew that you were paying an unnecessary tax, would you continue to pay it?

If you were overpaying a certain amount of tax, would you purposely overpay it?

If you could legally recapture or keep some of the money you pay in taxes, would you, do it?

If no one has taught or informed you of these techniques, I feel very sorry for you. It really is unfortunate.

The most common belief is that using a qualified plan is the best way to reduce your taxation. This is what you are told to believe. Don't be surprised to find out that this is not really true. The tax savings we are talking about here is not loading up the 401K Retirement Savings Account or the Individual Retirement Account (IRA) plans. It could be the total opposite.

A little bit of tax history. Our American forefathers in 1913 passed the sixteenth amendment allowing the federal government to impose an income tax on the hard working people of this great country.

But it was only supposed to be a temporary tax. A hundred and eight years later, taxes still exist. I don't think it's temporary anymore.

The Federal Reserve began, and 213 banks joined, the President Wilson gave his very first State of the Union Address, the American Cancer Society was founded.

In 1933, my father was born in Caposele, Italy! The Federal Deposit Insurance Corporation (FDIC) was created under the authority of the Federal Reserve Act.

1943 was the year that the three month treasury bill average return was 0.37% with a six percent inflation. and the greatest depression ended in the USA conversion to the war economy and a dramatic increase in employment.

In 1953, The New York Yankees won four games to two over the Brooklyn Dodgers, 4.14 percent T-bonds annual return, and the movie *Peter Pan* made its debut at the Famous the Theater, in New York City called the Roxy!

In 1964, the year of my birth, The Beatles released, "*I want to hold your hand,*" Rubella reached epidemic proportions in the USA; T-bonds were not at 3.73 percent annual return, and the Ford Motor Company introduced the Mustang!

In 1980, 25.77 percent S&P 500 annual yield without reinvestment, and the Dow Jones Industrial Average annual yield without reinvestment was at 14.93 percent.

In 1990, space shuttle Discovery places the Hubble Space Telescope into orbit, the MSCI World Index Fund total index annual change was -23.10%.

In 2000, The Russell 2000 total return annual was .08%. A judge rules Microsoft violated antitrust laws, maintained monopoly power, and the RIAA—The Recording Industry Assoc. of America—sued Napster, Inc in the first major case regarding copyrights and file sharing.

In 2010, the Census Bureau found record income inequality-gap between rich and poor; the widest ever; republicans won control of the House of Repetitive; gained six seats in Senate; won the majority of the state's governorships.

I share this information with you because all this information provides us answers that we are searching for regarding taxes and the future of taxes.

I welcome you to visit the following website and enjoy what you find. www.debtclock.org I look at this clock weekly, and I am frightened for the future of our country and government finances.

Tax Refunds:

I do not understand why any American would want a refund at the end of the tax year. I have explained this to my two children for years. I hope I got the message across to them. It's kind of like sitting on an airplane these days. There are so many different fares that someone can get. How would it make you feel if the person sitting next to you paid $300-$500 less than you? How would that make you feel? This is what you are exactly doing by overpaying your income taxes.

I want you to understand the destruction you could possibly be doing to yourself, relationships, and finances.

You get up and go to work every day for the majority of the year. You pay your taxes and more than you should if you are getting a refund. Have you ever said, "Hey, if we only had the money."

Well, if you didn't overpay, you may or could have had the extra dough!

You work already and pay your taxes, and at the end of the year, the government repays what they owe you.

Is there any interest on the back end because you were so kind to overpay your taxes? I didn't think so!

From the many different articles, I have read that the average American receives a $3,000 refund check. That is almost a car payment for you at $250 a month. Can or could this improve your standard of living?

The most important thing could be just adjusting your withholdings on your paycheck, which would provide you more liquidly!

CHAPTER 6

YOUR FUTURE

O ver the next 3,000 days, many things will be changing regarding our economy, rates of returns, taxes, and inflation. Here is where I would like for you to experience your defining moment to begin to understand the efficiency of money.

The concepts that I have discussed are simple yet effective methods of reducing and eliminating financial transfers of your wealth that you make every day without knowing.

The goal is also to help you through a different thought process that will make you think many layers deeper about your money.

A life-changing approach to how your money works. Knowledge is what you learn. Wisdom is the ability to apply that knowledge to your everyday life.

Many of the financial lessons that the average American uses today are based on what you have been told to think, not how to think. This philosophy has created a dilemma and a crisis for the average American family. Being told what to think involves you transferring your wealth to those who create these situations, control the outcome, and profit from you.

Most of the marketing materials that financial institutions share with you can be misguided and confusing, thereby, leaving you hanging high and dry. Traditional financial thinking is not a science. If it was, no one would ever lose money.

Others are controlling your financial success, and they provide you enough information to keep you in the game long enough until they have all the control.

Today the vast majority of people are troubled and confused about the economy, and they have been bombarded by the media, bullied by salespeople, and bewildered by the things they feel they need to know.

Everyone who takes the time to read and study the strategies that I have discussed in this book. It will enable you and your loved one to be in a better financial situation.

I really want you to think really deep here. If you have over $100,000 of equity in your home, what is it doing for you? What is the rate of return of the equity of your home?

Are you maximizing your 401K or retirement plan? Would you rather save on taxes today or save on taxes in the future? if you believe that taxes will be increasing in the years to come, what do you do?

If you have been given a choice to save and deposit your money in one of three buckets.

A   100%   income taxable

B   100%   Capital Gain Taxable

C   100%   tax free

Where would you deposit the money? Stop and think about which bucket you are depositing your dollars in. What benefits are you getting by using your present accounts, and what benefits could you also receive if you change your thought process?

What you know today will determine where you will be 5 to 10 years from now. You must be proactive, not reactive!

So many times, people say no to a question before I have even had the chance to ask it.

I always find it funny, because there may be an opportunity right in front of you, but you just don't see it. How can you say yes or no to ideas that you do not even know exist?

Are you humbling enough to accept the following?

1. You know what you know.   Ex. I know the sky is blue.

2. You know what you don't know.   Ex. I know I do not know how to fly a plane.

Your economic situation is a matter of choice, not a matter of chance. Misguided and self-inflicted, many decisions are made with the lack of knowledge driven by fear and cautious of change; your financial decisions are made by default, without knowledge and unaware of any unintended consequences.

Over the past several years, they have seen many financial lessons they learned to fail. them. They know they cannot live on four and five percent rates of return, yet they are scared and hesitant to make the crucial decisions necessary to survive in today's economy.

To make things worse, ninety million Americans are faced with the most critical financial challenge of their lives.

How do you break down this problem? How can you analyze it carefully? Once we do this, you will have all the information and a very clear choice of what is available to you to help keep more of your wealth from being eroded. As I said earlier, the decisions you make today WILL determine where you will be 5 - 10 years from now. Be confident in your decision!

CHAPTER 7

OWNING YOUR OWN HOME

This could be the greatest transfer of wealth that you will never see coming. Isn't it the American dream to own your home? This dream could also become a nightmare fast without you having any control of the outcome. Buying the best home for you at the least amount is the goal. But when you purchase the home, you also have to take other considerations into factor, like taxes and home insurance. Then comes all the fun of the upkeep, to get comfortable in the mighty home you purchased.

Many of us have worked for years and years to save enough money for the down payment. Now that you have saved enough for the down payment comes the fun of applying for a home loan. But which one is right for you? Then you need to produce all of the income pay stubs, tax returns, line of credits, and then the final piece of the puzzle, the "Credit Score."

Now, don't you think it is odd that they did not ask you for most of that information when you wanted to deposit money in their bank? In all honesty, the bankants to protect their behind and make sure you are creditworthy of getting a loan for your home. We all must prove without a doubt that we are good standing credit risk and qualify so we can afford this new home that we want.

There are many different types of mortgage companies that you can select from, even online. You can begin to look for the best mortgage company. There is fifteen years, twenty years, and thirty years fixed mortgages. There are also many other different ones that you can inquire about with your mortgage professional. No matter which mortgage you feel is best for you, there will be a transfer of money.

These companies understand that buying a home is not the sale price but the affordability of your monthly mortgage payment. Did you stop and look at the final price of your home at the end of the loan? It's just like what the car companies do every day.

It is complex and confusing. In all of the uncertainty in purchasing a home, there are secrets that very few are aware of. We have been told that owning a home is one of the largest and best investments we will ever make. If that were not true, when would you want to know about it?

There are important questions that need to be discussed. Questions like: Is a home a good place to keep your money? What is the rate of return of the equity in your home? Should you pay your home off as fast as you can?

Discovering these answers that may surprise you!

With more information, you will have the ability to make better life financial decisions that could impact generations to come after you are long gone.

I believe that everyone should have their home paid off and paid off as fast as possible.

We need to separate fact from fiction so you can learn to pay off your home in the most efficient way possible.

Let's take a quiz: True or False

1. A large down payment will save you more money on your mortgage over time than a small down payment?

2. A fifteen-year mortgage will save more money over time than a thirty-year mortgage.

3. Making extra principal payments saves you money?

4. Is the interest rate the main factor in determining the cost of a mortgage?

5. You are more secure having your home paid off than financing one hundred percent?

If you answered true to any of the above five questions, please keep reading. If you answered false, proceed to the next chapter.

Most mortgage contracts are based on the payment amount and interest rate. While these factors are important, several other factors must be considered. Things like inflation, tax deductions, how much of down payment, opportunity costs.

To help understand how these factors might ultimately impact you, I will introduce you to three fictitious couples.

3 couples example

Each couple has the same goal. Having their home paid off. They each believe that their method is the best.

Couple #1, let's call them the Mr. & Mrs. Free and Clear. They have paid off their mortgage, and they have no monthly payments.

Couple #2 Mr. & Mrs. Owe it Alls. They could have paid cash for the home like the Free and Clears but decided to keep their money and invest in a safe account so they could access it in case they ever needed it. Although they owe it all to their mortgage, they have no other debt.

Couple #3 Mr. & Mrs. Pay Extra. Each month they make extra payments, to pay off as soon as possible.

So, which of these couples do you think is in the best position? Let's explore several other mortgage factors to find out they impact our couples.

One area many people tend to forget and factor in when getting a mortgage, is inflation. If you have a fixed payment today at $2,000 a month, what will that same $2,000 a month buy for you over the next ten, twenty, or thirty years? Assuming an inflation rate of three percent, $2,000 over the next thirty years, it will only have the ability to purchase $823 worth of goods.

Let's apply this example to what it means to you and your mortgage. Making a fixed mortgage payment of $2,000 a month today feels like $2,000. But in thirty years, it will feel like you will only be paying $823 per month. So, the early mortgage payments that you may feel much more painful in the beginning. The reason is that they are your most valuable dollars today.

So, let's check in on the couples.

The Free and Clear gave their most valuable dollars to the bank upfront.

The Pay Extras voluntarily gave the bank their best dollars, on top of their required mortgage payment every chance they get.

The Owe It Alls have a monthly mortgage payment that allows them to give the bank payments worth less and less each month while keeping their money protected and invested while potentially offsetting the impact of inflation.

The concept: Your home costs you more the faster you pay it off because you are doing so with your most valuable dollars.

Most people make a large down payment to reduce the mortgage payment and to save interest. The question that I ask is does your down payment earn you any interest? NO. This loss is called the dreaded Lost Opportunity Cost.

Key Concept #2

Opportunity Cost: If you lose a dollar that you did not have to lose, you not only lose that dollar, but you also lose what that dollar could have earned for you had you been able to keep it!

What would the Free n Clears down payment be worth if they had been able to keep it and invest it? Let's put some math behind this concept and take a deeper look.

Let's make the following assumptions: All three couples purchased a $300,000 home.

	Down payment	Monthly Extra	Extra Payment	Investment Account
#1	$300,000	0	0	0
#2	$60,000	$1500	$1000	0
#3	0	$2000	0	$300,000

The Free and Clear's made the largest down payment possible. Which was all of their $300,000

The Pay Extras did not have enough upfront so they accelerated the principal payment by extra each month.

The Owe it All's has the least amount down and financed it as long as possible.

Assuming. An interest rate of eight percent. Again, I want to stress this is for illustration purposes only.

The Owe It All's $300,000 could have grown to $3,018,797 in thirty years. If they could borrow the $300,000 at a lower rate, they would keep the difference.

The Free n Clears $300,000 down payment earns no interest.

So, if the Free n Clears cannot sell their home in thirty years for $3,018,797, They made just a minor financial error.

Investment Opportunities

Rather than paying cash, the Owe it All's, saved and invested their entire $300,000, so now they must make monthly mortgage payments. However, the interest portion of their payments are tax-deductible, this deduction reduces the cost of borrowing significantly.

The Free N Clears, on the other hand, paid their entire $300,000 down and gave away the control of the money to the bank, and they are now ready to invest the after-tax monthly amount they would have otherwise given the mortgage company.

However, since they have no mortgage interest deductions, they would have to assume higher investment risk than the Owe It Alls.

So, with the understanding that money used for down payments earns no interest and is controlled by the bank, and reduces tax deductions, what is the ideal amount to put down when purchasing a home? NOTHING.

Key Concept:

Remember, if you finance, you transfer interest to the lending institutions for the privilege of using their money. If you pay cash, you save interest expense, but you lose interest income , because that money is not earning anything for you. The money in your home earns zero.

Your home as an investment

Most people today consider their home one of their largest investments. Let's see if this is a good place to put your money.

Assume the Free N Clears home is worth $300,000 today, and they bought their home seven years ago for $229,000 and added about $25,000 in improvements on their home. Their rate of Return would be in the neighborhood of 2.41 percent. Would you consider this a good return?

Appreciation

You may be thinking we forgot that your home is appreciating. Let's assume all three couples have the same value of their homes, $300,000. Whose home will appreciate the fastest? The fact is, they will all appreciate the same. Making large down payments or making extra monthly payments does not make your home worth more than it's present value.

Key Concept

Your home appreciates the same whether you have paid it off or financed one hundred percent.

Net cost to borrow equals your loan rate less your tax bracket. If you receive a mortgage interest deduction, it reduces the investment risk you have to earn on your money for you to be in control!

CHAPTER 8

TIME TO TALK OPEN AND HONESTLY:

I t's time for us to talk honestly and openly; this is not to blame the other political party, or another institution. This isn't a sales pitch or rant. It's about getting to the point, for real.

This is about a discussion about your and my financial life. Yes, your and my personal life, because I am in the same boat as you, and how our financial success is being confiscated without any evidence of a crime.

The perpetrators that are making our lives difficult are the ones that control the rules yet continue to put us at risk every day. Yet, they have the nerve to advise us on how we should be living our lives.

You see, many of you already know this. I don't believe in traditional financial thinking, how it is being sold to the American public. It would not be a science. If it was truly a science, no one would ever lose money.

The results of traditional thinking lie somewhere between the loss of hope and hopelessness. Because the problem is common sense keeps getting in the way of this type of thinking.

You have to understand that we are involved in the evolution of transferring away most of our wealth to those that control the situation, control the outcomes, and profit from it. Yet, we continue to rely on the steadiness, and the trustworthiness, of the government and financial services industry to guide us to our futures. Unfortunately, these two groups create the most transfers of wealth in our lives.

I believe I have the leverage to make things happen in our business. I believe in the wisdom and not necessarily product. In traditional thinking, stability is often an illusion, and you may discover that hope is not a good strategy.

Financial marketing should be about the ability to change everyday lives. If you recall, not long ago—six to eight years ago—we watched good, hard working people lose their homes and some of their retirement dreams from a distance. And in that historical moment, we finally discovered the lack of understanding about the economic trends and shifts, and how they impact people's lives.

The reality is that the only thing that traditional financial thinking predicts is the financial loss that people face due to taxes, inflation, and depreciation of the dollar.

The average American family household is undisciplined, unready, and in many cases unaware they are in a battle for their financial future.

I have been asking in my meetings with clients this: I want you to think about it. Besides Covid-19, what in the last decade has the government and financial services industry done to improve the life of the average American?

What are the challenges you are facing on an everyday basis? What are the myths and reality behind traditional thinking and trying to solve some of the problems they face?

Knowing is all well and good, but you need to put all the knowledge to work.

I believe in the following:

1. I can increase someone's life now by increasing what they know.

2. That the government has seriously infringed on my financial future.

3. What I know today will determine where I will be –five to ten years from now.

4. What I know is scary, but what someone doesn't know can be disastrous.

5. That traditional thinking fails to reach its financial goals.

6. The next 1000 days will be critical to our nation.

7. The family remains one of the most powerful financial tools.

8. We continue to feed the problem instead of solving the problem.

9. I can make a difference.

CHAPTER 9

FACTORS THAT "ERODE" OUR WEALTH

Creating wealth, many people believe, is very simple. Yet, a majority of Americans from what I have seen in the typical American family of two income household between 95,000 - $120,000, two to three children ages between ages three and seven, and at least one pet, have less than six months of liquid savings in liquid account in the event of emergencies. I am so uncomfortable and afraid for them. You see, now I know and understand the risk that I took because I was in their shoes at one time. They are one major injury, one major economic mishap, and premature death from complete financial disaster. It is my job to explain it to them if they are in this predicament and do not realize it.

When I ask them how they feel about being in such a pinch, living paycheck to paycheck, they respond, we understand the risk, but we are trying to get ourselves out of this situation.

Most of us have a junk drawer in our home. Some may have more than one. I call these people hoarders and junk collectors. Joking.

These draws contain a bunch of stuff that is in them. Most of the time, those items are used one for things only. A single use of that particular item. Kind of like the bag of air in packing boxes. Only one use.

People also make money decisions one at a time. They have purchased financial products that are being used for a single use, and benefit. They purchase financial products that are rarely looked at or reviewed, and if they are looked at, they look at the total present balance. They do nothing about if they are satisfied with it or not.

Another example is your car insurance. It is purchased to protect your asset, which is your vehicle. They purchase the auto policy and put it away, and many times never review those policies for years.

Many of these decisions that have been made were purchased at a certain time, with no coordination or integration to their financial plan.

In introducing my potential clients to my process, I help the organize, and coordinate their assets. Once I have this done, we can view these assets to see if we can integrate, to maximize the efficiency of the dollars they have worked so hard for. We can look at their entire financial position on one single sheet of paper. Making it very simple to understand. Here we look at the five areas of a person's financial life:

1. Personal family information. Age, income, children's ages.

2. We look at their cash flow or lack of. Their list of debts. Balances, payments, and interest on these debts.

3. Protection. We review and discuss how the individuals are protecting their assets, their income, and their lives. These are all insurance products.

4. Savings. We pinpoint balances of all savings accounts, interests rates on earnings, and the they type of savings regarding tax deferred or tax free.

5. Growth areas: In this area is the higher risk, but where we give up control of our money in hopes that we can generate a larger rate of return, such as stocks, bonds, muni bonds, and so forth.

6. As we begin to generate and create wealth, we must also look at areas that can help us protect from losing it to outside forces such as taxes, inflation law suit, and bankruptcies, and the silent one! Lost Opportunity Cost. (L.O.C)

Taxes:

My disclaimer: I am in no way suggesting any legal tax advice. This is strictly an explanation of how taxes can and will erode our wealth.

What taxes do we pay? Most individuals think of these: income, state income tax in most states, capital gains tax. But there are many taxes that we pay on a daily basis. These are sales tax, gasoline tax, cigarette tax, alcohol tax, gaming tax, etc.

Not only do we pay these taxes every day, but these taxes are always fluctuating and mostly fluctuating in the upward direction. A major reason is the social government programs that have been established through the years. Remember, in 1912, there were no taxes, and in 1913, when they imposed taxes, it was only temporary. So temporary has lasted nearly 110 years to date, with no end. So much for temporary.

A tax that is deferred to a later date in time is a potential tax at a much higher rate than it is today. Over the past twenty-fve years, we have had one of the lowest taxes in modern history. We discuss the three things that could happen in the future to taxes, down, stay the same, or go up, and the response is, you guessed it Up. Then there is the tax-free area, here your asset has the potential to grow tax free. But the government is the one that makes the rules here, and the more affluent American family with a combined income of $_____ or more cannot take advantage of this because of their income because they are successful and good wage earners.

We must all have a fundamental financial strategy that will assist us in preventing or minimizing the offertory of paying these taxes. If we do not have a properly designed strategy, our money will most definitely be eroded over time to taxes.

INFLATION:

We will discuss this, but very few of us have a clear understanding of how inflation will erode our money over time. Today, if you have an annual income of $100,000, add inflation of 3% yearly, twenty years from now, to maintain the income level of $100,000, you will NEED $180,611 to equal today's $100,000. At 4% inflation you will need to have an income of $219,112 to equal $100,000 today. But a majority will never use the inflation factor in the equation to accumulate wealth.

An example would be, what can you not buy today for $1 that you could have bought last year. We present, in 2021 a fast-food chain is promoting any size drink for $1.59. In 2019 it was advertising the same drink for $1. Over two-year, that is a thirty percent rate of inflation.

Another example thanks to Robert Castiglione for helping me understand inflation by using the "Oranges." If you and I were both holding four oranges mathematically, it would add up to eight. Now, if we were to leave the room, lock it from anyone taking the oranges for twenty years, and we both returned, we would still have the oranges totaling eight, but they have eroded over time. We would not eat them, would we? NO WAY…. That is an invisible eroding factor. Thanks, Bob!

People will say that for our money to keep pace with inflation, our money needs to grow at the same rate on an annual basis. If not, you will lose the purchasing power of that money.

LOST OPPORTUNITY COST:

Have you ever said to yourself, I wish I should have? I wish we could have? I wish we did? You are describing lost opportunity cost. You understand what L.O.C is but never had it explained to you that way before.

Have you ever lost money by accident? How did you feel? Did it put a knot in your belly?

Assuming it did. What did you lose? Not only did you lose the money, but if you had saved them money in the market, you would have potentially lost all the interest you could have earned. But just not today, but you have incurred the L.O.C for the rest of your lifetime. Many of us never calculate this when it comes to wealth generation and an additional eroding factor.

Lost Opportunity Cost needs to be understood. What is (L.O.C)? L.O.C is one that most financial advisors do not use when calculating a client's financial plan. Without considering the (L.O.C) in your mathematical calculations, you will most defiantly not have an accurate total in the future.

A vast majority of people have never been taught about the latter. Most of us including myself, were never taught in school how to grow, and protect our assets to grow more efficiently. How do we safeguard it for taxes and inflation?

Let me begin by reminding you of two symbols. The + and the ×. They each are very important in math and economics. We add our money together to get a sum, but we must multiply our money to help it grow, but not only grow but to grow it faster. As we get it to grow, we must now protect it from the eroding factors.

CHAPTER 10

FINANCIAL CLARITY

The most important asset that you have is time. Your time is more valuable than the money you have. People need to understand that it is the only consistent element in your life. Some people are going to have more time, some are going to have enough time, some will run out of time, and some will have too much time. As I mentioned, this is the only consistent element in your life. You will spend all your time. I promise you that.

As the Beatles would say, time moves within you, time moves with you. So, no matter what you do, take a course of action in traditional financial thinking or don't, time continues to move.

What we must understand is that we will all spend the time that we have. We can't stop time. Once you lose it you can never get it back. The main question is, how much time do you have?

In the financial world time is the only element that is consistently correct.

T × R × M = Accumulation. Let me say this again, time is the only consistent formula that is correct, in this equation.

Very put without time, money cannot compound.

Here is example 1:

Your working years thirty i.e. 360 months

$100 in thirty years at five percent = $446.77 (Projected and assumed) M x R x T = Wealth

Example 2

If two months in every year, the money didn't compound you would have a total of $348, not $447. A 22% (lost time = lost money.) And $348 if taxed at twenty percent and inflation at three percent, in thirty years has the buying power of $115 today.

How do we bridge the gap on that? How do we make up for the time that we lost?

Can we use someone else's time to reach our desired results if we don't have enough? I want you to think about what I just asked. Can you use someone else's time to get where you want to go?

We need to understand and discover and create time leverage. Time leverage is about using the least amount of money to create the most wealth using the least amount of time. This should be everyone's goal. Time is more powerful than money.

CHAPTER 11

THE MONEY MATRIX

Understanding how money works, you need to apply a litmus test to measure the effectiveness and usefulness of your money. It is important to remember that way too much emphasis is put on the rate of return, mentally and too little on how money can work for you.

There are a number of categories that the money you have right now can fall into. You can have IRAs, 401Ks, Roth IRAs, defined Benefits programs, SEPs, mutual funds, bank savings, CDs, stocks, bonds, homes, real estate, business, and life insurance.

You may be able to think of more, but these are the most general categories of money that you may have. Take each of these categories, list them in a column, and ask yourself the following questions, of each of your money categories. You will discover the efficiency, effectiveness, and safety of the money you have.

Risk:

Does this category or the type of money involve risk? Can you lose money? Are mutual funds and stocks subject to losses? Can your bank saving program lose money? There is different degrees of risk. Some things may have a higher degree of risk than others.

So, when it comes to each mark, each with one "H" for High Risk, "M" for Medium Risk, "L" Low Risk. If this category or type of money has no risk, write "none" as the risk questions all the types of money you have.

Guarantees:

Does this category or type of money offer guarantees? Has this money assured you of controlled positive results in the future? Does your IRA have guarantees? Does the mutual fund that you own have any guarantee?

Penalties:

Does this category or type of money have penalties associated with it? This is a very important question that needs to be asked and understood; many types of your money might have penalties for early withdrawal of an IRA? Are there penalties for not withdrawing enough out of your IRA during retirement? How about early withdrawals out of your bank CD?

Use and Control:

Is your money liquid? Can you get it when you need it? Do you have the ability to use it? Answering simply in a yes or no will give you a much clearer view of whether you control this type of money category.

Protected:

If you were to get sued, what types of money would be protected against lawsuits? The money you have in the bank? The equity of your home? Your investment accounts? Your 401K, is so important to know and understand. Many people are great risk takers, yet they do not know this.

Leverage:

Does this type of money create the most amount of money for the least amount you invest? How do you achieve this in real estate? Former President Donald Trump uses this exact money strategy in most of his business real estate deals.

Tax Deferred:

Very few things in our lifetime escape taxation. Many types of money are taxed on their growth on an annual basis. A bank CD, for example. Is this true of your 401K or your traditional IRA? No, these are tax-deferred. These are taxed when you take them out or begin the distribution. Then you could potentially be taxed at a higher tax rate. HUMMMM

Tax Free:

Does this type of money have to get distributed to you or your heirs, your family, tax free in the event of something happening to you? Is an IRA tax free? How about a bank CD, bank savings plan? Mutual funds tax free? On your chart, list the types of money you can have tax free at distribution. You will be surprised at what you can discover.

Collateral:

Sometimes lending institutions will grant loans if there is some collateral or hard asset involved. A home could be used as collateral for a loan, but how about an IRA or a 401K? Can mutual funds be used as collateral? Collateral typically has relatively safe value and assures a lending institution of controlling value while lending your money.

Disability Benefits:

In the event of an illness or accident in your life, will this type of category of money continue to make deposits or payments for you while you are disabled? Will your company continue to make your 401K deposits for you even if you are not working? Will your investment broker continue to make monthly payments or deposits into your account for you while you are injured or sick? Will, the company that you are dealing with deposit or make payments for this type of money? Yes, or no?

Wealth Transfers:

In your death, how will this type of money you have been taxed or transferred to the next generation of family members or heir? Will someone else have to pay the tax on your IRA if you die? Do you have this type of money to create real tax-free wealth for your family, kids, or heirs? Apply this question to all the types of your money. Simple yes or no.

CHAPTER 12

2 SPECIFIC TYPES OF WEALTH

Statement Wealth

What is statement wealth? Do you understand? Where do you find it?

As you walk towards your mailbox or sit in front of your computer to log into your accounts portal to either open or download your bank statement, your credit card statements, along with the IRA, 401K, Roth Statements. The first thing most of us do is look at that balance! How much do I have? How much did I earn? How much did I lose?

This could be a very emotional rollercoaster for many of us because these statements represent the hard work you have done or are doing to help you accumulate your hard-earned dollars for one day of enjoyment during your golden years.

What questions come to your mind when you are reviewing your statements?

As I begin to look at mine, I ask myself the following regarding every account I own. How much control did I have over the outcome, and how will I be taxed? These are so important to consider, yet many people I have assisted in my professional career have never considered these types of questions regarding their accounts.

Remember that you made the choices of where to save and invest your money. You still didn't have control over the result. You are just holding a simple statement that you received in the mail or download from your portal.

Contractual Wealth:

Now, this kind of wealth is so exciting. Contractual wealth indicates there is a contract or some form of legal document in place. When you enter into a contract, there has been some form of negotiation or agrees to financial terms on a deal. This wealth needs much more thought than the statement wealth we discussed a little earlier.

This could be why most people never fully achieve wealth in this type of wealth.

When you enter into a contract with a business or someone, it means that if you do your part, the other party has a legal obligation to fulfill the deal. If either party cannot complete the negotiated contract for some reason, then either party has recourse rights.

So like earlier, you go to get your statements in your mailbox, or you download your online statements, and you begin to see that the Acme Fund Company reported to you that you lost forty to fifty percent of your value due to a market correction. Now think about calling the company and asking them to refund you the forty to fifty percent loss. No, that's funny. The reason I say this for this example you have no recourse of control.

Having contractual wealth offers a more predictable path of designing the life your desire in retirement. The kind of wealth typically allows for greater benefits, control of returns and taxation, thus providing a greater sense of peace during the crazy roller coaster ride, and trying to time the market. So, as we examine new or old opportunities, think through these concepts of statement wealth vs. contractual wealth. You have a much better position if you have some or more contractual wealth on your side of the balance sheet!

CONCLUSION

Learning how your money works will result in an *AH HA* moment, but in many cases, you will need support and assistance when planning and fully understanding a sound financial thought process.

Find a competent professional to help you is sometimes the most difficult. Many professionals have the misfortune of not knowing what they should know.

Traditional thinking will result in traditional results, which is not good enough in today's financial world.

It is very important to find someone who has been exposed to the understanding of how money works.

If a professional has forwarded this book to you, they are aware of the value of its content. He may be the professional that is willing to take the time to educate you and teach you how money works.

Seek out experience and knowledge from a professional that does more than push financial products. Find a professional that you are comfortable with to develop a long-lasting relationship with them. We have discussed many professionals who have taken the time and have been exposed to the thought process. It has become a valuable tool for them with tremendous results for their clients and potentially for you!

I wish you all the blessings the Lord wants to provide for you, and always remember that you can accomplish all things through Christ.

Ducci